CMS Made Simple 1.9
Beginner's Guide: LITE

Get started with CMS Made Simple by learning how to
create pages and navigation for a professional website

Sofia Hauschildt

[PACKT] open source
PUBLISHING   community experience distilled

BIRMINGHAM - MUMBAI

CMS Made Simple 1.9

Beginner's Guide: LITE

First published: April 2011

Production Reference: 2200411

Published by Packt Publishing Ltd.
32 Lincoln Road
Olton
Birmingham, B27 6PA, UK.

ISBN 978-1-849516-40-2

www.packtpub.com

Cover Image by Vinayak Chittar (vinayak.chittar@gmail.com)

Credits

Author

Sofia Hauschildt

Reviewers

Jeremy Bass

Yury V. Zaytsev

Acquisition Editor

Sarah Cullington

Technical Editors

Hithesh Uchil

Indexer

Hemangini Bari

Production Coordinator

Kruthika Bangera

Cover Work

Kruthika Bangera

About the Author

Sofia Hauschildt is a web mastering and web development tutor, who started designing and developing professional websites in 1995 just before her graduation in Computer Science. With experience as a data warehouse developer and ERP consultant, she became a self-employed tutor. During her career, she has been contracted by IT and management academies, the German army, several city administrations, and international companies such as Siemens. Her work as a tutor is always focused on practical training combined with a theoretical background in order to get fast and handy results.

I would like to express my gratitude to all those who gave me the possibility to complete this book. I want to thank my husband Jens for investing a huge amount of time in the first reviews of this book and his patient love. Furthermore, I have to thank Yury V. Zaytsev for his stimulating support and interesting discussions.

A special thanks goes to my parents who encouraged me to go ahead with this book and gave me incredible mental support.

About the Reviewers

Jeremy Bass began learning web construction at the age of 12 using the "view source" on sites such as the young Yahoo and the late GeoCities. Armed with a computer and a talent for the fine arts, he has been in computer-based graphics ever since. A few of the high points are stents at an international telescope (Gemini in Hawaii) and winning a Telly award for 3D animation. Currently, Jeremy works with Digital Barn Productions in Idaho, and Defined Clarity in Philadelphia along with freelancing and participation in the CMSMS community.

> I would like to thank my wife, Aimee, for understanding I work long hours not just to grow, but for her and the kids. This was fun.

Yury V. Zaytsev has an advanced degree in physics from the Nizhny Novgorod State University, Russia, and is currently working towards his doctorate in Computational Neuroscience at the University of Freiburg, Germany. Yury's primary interests concern scientific computing, modeling, and simulation, particularly of the complex dynamics of large populations of neurons.

Yury's first contact with computers was at the age of 6 when he programmed his first text-based role-playing game in BASIC on a historical 80386 machine. This inspired a never ending passion for programming, which also led to a brief career at the age of 17 in freelance web development for companies in Russia, Europe, and overseas.

Having successfully implemented many commercial and hobby projects with CMS Made Simple, Yury is happy to contribute to the widespread adoption of CMSMS for the benefit of both users and developers.

Table of Contents

Preface

CMS Made Simple is an open source content management system that allows rapid website development in a fraction of the normal time, while avoiding hours of coding by providing modules and third-party add-ons. With this book in hand, you will be able to harness the power of this modular and extensible content management system at your fingertips.

This guide for CMS Made Simple is based on practical and working solutions allowing you to understand how this powerful and simple application can support you in your daily work. This book covers the basics from setting up CMS Made Simple to creating pages and navigation

This is a step-by-step case study, aimed at helping you to learn the basics of CMS Made Simple and to prepare you to build a complete professional website.

This book is a LITE edition of a longer book, CMS Made Simple 1.6 Beginner's Guide. With the full edition, you are guided through the creation of a fully functional, professional website, and you'll learn how to lay it out, use core modules, and set roles and permissions for your visitors. This edition is updated for CMSMS version 1.9 and walks you through the first stages of creating a site with CMS Made Simple so that you will have installed the software and be able to create pages and navigation.

To find out more about upgrading to the full edition, visit www.packtpub. com/liteupgrade and log into your account for offers and help. If you don't have an account on PacktPub.com, visit today and set one up!

What this book covers

Chapter 1, Building Websites with CMS Made Simple introduces a website with its functional requirements.

Chapter 2, Getting Started explains how to install CMS Made Simple, how its admin console is organized, and how to configure CMS Made Simple for sending out e-mails.

Chapter 3, Creating Pages and Navigation focuses on creating, editing, and organizing pages. It introduces the page hierarchy and search engine friendly URLs. At the end of this chapter, you will have the complete page structure for the case study website.

Appendix, Pop Quiz Answers contains the answers to the pop quizzes throughout the book.

What you need for this book

CMS Made Simple is a PHP application that uses a MySQL database. This means that you need a web hosting with PHP and MySQL to run CMS Made Simple. You can install a web server on your local PC for testing environments and/or on the remote web hosting for live websites. The requirements for CMS Made Simple are as follows:

◆ Web server on Linux/Unix or Windows 2000/XP/ME/2003 or OS X

◆ PHP 5.2.4+ for core versions after 1.7, though PHP 5.2.12+ is highly recommended:

  ❑ `safe_mode` should be off

  ❑ At least 16 MB of available memory for PHP

  ❑ PHP tokenizer support enabled

  ❑ At least one of ImageMagick or GDlib enabled

◆ MySQL 4.1+ or PostgreSQL 7+

◆ Enough access to your server to upload files and change some permissions

Who this book is for

This book is perfect for newcomers as well as webmasters who are looking for an introduction to building powerful and professional websites with a content management system. Basic knowledge of HTML and CSS is the only requirement. The workshop covers all aspects of web publishing and is aimed at, editors, and web managers.

Conventions

In this book, you will find several headings appearing frequently.

To give clear instructions of how to complete a procedure or task, we use:

Time for action – heading

1. Action 1
2. Action 2
3. Action 3

Instructions often need some extra explanation so that they make sense, so they are followed with:

What just happened?

This heading explains the working of tasks or instructions that you have just completed.

You will also find some other learning aids in the book, including:

Pop quiz – heading

These are short multiple choice questions intended to help you test your own understanding.

Have a go hero – heading

These set practical challenges and give you ideas for experimenting with what you have learned.

You will also find a number of styles of text that distinguish between different kinds of information. Here are some examples of these styles, and an explanation of their meaning.

Code words in text are shown as follows: "Your root directory can be `public_html` (or `wwwroot` or `htdocs`), please ask your provider if you are not sure where to upload the files."

New terms and **important words** are shown in bold. Words that you see on the screen, in menus or dialog boxes for example, appear in the text like this: "Open **My First Style Sheet** from the list of stylesheets (**Layout | Stylesheets**) for edit."

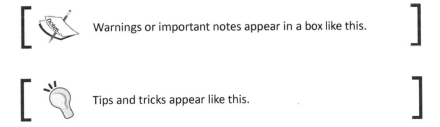

Warnings or important notes appear in a box like this.

Tips and tricks appear like this.

Reader feedback

Feedback from our readers is always welcome. Let us know what you think about this book—what you liked or may have disliked. Reader feedback is important for us to develop titles that you really get the most out of.

To send us general feedback, simply send an e-mail to `feedback@packtpub.com`, and mention the book title via the subject of your message.

If there is a book that you need and would like to see us publish, please send us a note in the **SUGGEST A TITLE** form on www.packtpub.com or e-mail suggest@packtpub.com. If there is a topic that you have expertise in and you are interested in either writing or contributing to a book on, see our author guide on www.packtpub.com/authors.

Customer support

Now that you are the proud owner of a Packt book, we have a number of things to help you to get the most from your purchase.

Errata

Although we have taken every care to ensure the accuracy of our content, mistakes do happen. If you find a mistake in one of our books—maybe a mistake in the text or the code—we would be grateful if you would report this to us. By doing so, you can save other readers from frustration and help us improve subsequent versions of this book. If you find any errata, please report them by visiting http://www.packtpub.com/support, selecting your book, clicking on the **let us know** link, and entering the details of your errata. Once your errata are verified, your submission will be accepted and the errata will be uploaded on our website, or added to any list of existing errata, under the Errata section of that title. Any existing errata can be viewed by selecting your title from http://www.packtpub.com/support.

Piracy

Piracy of copyright material on the Internet is an ongoing problem across all media. At Packt, we take the protection of our copyright and licenses very seriously. If you come across any illegal copies of our works, in any form, on the Internet, please provide us with the location address or website name immediately so that we can pursue a remedy.

Please contact us at copyright@packtpub.com with a link to the suspected pirated material.

We appreciate your help in protecting our authors, and our ability to bring you valuable content.

Questions

You can contact us at questions@packtpub.com if you are having a problem with any aspect of the book, and we will do our best to address it.

1

Building Websites with CMS Made Simple

You already have some experience in creating websites with HTML and CSS and you know that you do not need any special software to create websites. However, if the website starts growing or your customers have more and more changes for the existing homepage, you wish you could automate some tasks like adding a new page to the website or slight changes in the design without having to edit every HTML file. CMS helps you to apply any change throughout the website with minimal efforts. It saves your time and reduces repeating tasks.

If you're holding this book in your hand, then it means that you are going to build a website with a CMS. A CMS is a complex application that works in the background and helps to separate different tasks while creating and running websites. Those tasks can include:

◆ Designing and laying out the website
◆ Implementing different website functionalities
◆ Writing and publishing content
◆ Analyzing and promoting the website

When creating websites with pure HTML and CSS, you usually mix logic, presentation, and content within the same code. However, this is time consuming and inflexible. For example, after adding additional navigation items or changing the year of copyright in the footer section of the page, you have to synchronize the changes made in every HTML file. Your customers may not be able to manage the content of their websites by themselves, as they would need HTML knowledge to do it. The solution to all the issues listed is a step towards content management system.

So let's get started with it...

What is a CMS?

CMS is an abbreviation for **content management system**. Generally, it is an application that helps to create a website structure and manage its content. By content, we mean any type of documents such as pages, images, structured data as products or users, and so on.

The most important goal of any CMS is the strict separation of content, design, and programming. You do not need to understand how a CMS is programmed when you write and publish the content. You do not need to be a web designer to create new pages and organize them into the navigation of the website. A programmer creates functionalities. A designer creates a layout without knowing how the program code is written and what exactly the content of every page will be. The editor uses the functions supplied by the programmer. The written content is automatically pasted into the layout created by the designer. That's it! Everyone does the job he/she can do best.

Typically, a CMS is used to offer the ability to manage the content of the website without any programming knowledge. The webmaster uses the CMS to create websites for customers who would like to manage their content by themselves. Once the design is made and the functionality is implemented, the customer can start entering his/her content. He/she does not care about anything else. He/she uses a graphical user interface to manage the content that is wrapped into the design.

A CMS consists of files and, in the case of CMS Made Simple, a database. Files provide functions that can retrieve any data from the database: content, design, features, and so on. The data retrieved is then wrapped as HTML and sent to the client (browser), because your visitors do not care how your website is made.

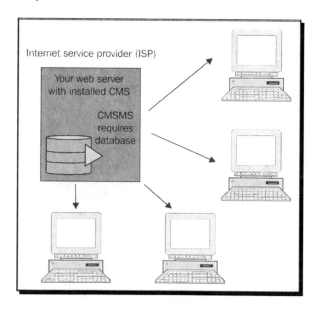

In the last image, you see a client-server structure. The server is your web space where the CMS is installed along with the database. Clients are visitors to your website. This means that to run a CMS, especially CMS Made Simple, you need some web space where you can create a new database and install CMS Made Simple. We will install CMS Made Simple step-by-step in the next chapter.

A CMS versus a website builder

A CMS is not a website builder. A website builder is used by people who would like to build websites without learning the technical aspects of web page production. They use ready-made design templates and select from the limited functions that the website builder offers. This kind of website production is inflexible and is often used to build private pages. A CMS caters to professional webmasters who create an individual website's layout and integrate any features that a customer needs.

Why CMS Made Simple?

You have decided to build a website with CMS Made Simple. Good choice! CMS Made Simple has several advantages:

♦ It's free for personal and commercial use.

♦ It's simple. You won't need more than half an hour to introduce your customer to the usage of the CMS. It is mostly intuitive.

♦ It's flexible in design. Any design that is created in HTML and CSS can be ported to CMS Made Simple. There are no restrictions.

♦ It's modular. The basic functionality of CMS Made Simple can be extended by installing over 100 additional modules that are offered for free on the official website.

♦ It's popular. You are not alone. A large international community helps you to solve your individual issues. Thousands of websites are already built using CMS Made Simple, so you are not going to be alone.

♦ It's open source. You can create your own functionality the way you need.

You can avoid provider lock-in to a certain proprietary closed source CMS solution. If a provider of proprietary software decides to charge you more, goes out of business, or does not want to incorporate desired new functionalities, then there's nothing you can do. With an Open Source CMS, if you face a problem that you can't solve on your own, you can at least hire a programmer who will solve it for you.

Preparing for installation

First of all, gather the details required for the installation of CMS Made Simple. You will need to know the following:

Data	Your value
Domain (website address)	http://
FTP host	
FTP user	
FTP password	
Database host address	
Database port (optional)	
Database name*	
Database username	
Database password	

*You have to create an empty database before you start the installation. It depends on your hosting as to how the new database can be created. Generally, a database can be created in the admin panel of your web hosting. Ask your provider for help if you face any difficulties.

All the information listed in the table should be available before you start the installation. Missing any of this information will make the installation of CMS Made Simple impossible. The information requested can be obtained from your hosting's support. Figure out and write down all the required access data now. You will need it during the setup and configuration process.

To start with the setup of CMS Made Simple on your web hosting, your domain should be registered and connected. Test it now. Open your browser, and give your domain name in the address bar. OK? If not, your domain provider will help you to solve any issues.

Browser

You can use any browser to manage CMS Made Simple, except Internet Explorer 6. This browser is pretty old. It was released in August, 2001 and does not meet the requirements of the modern Internet. Nevertheless, visitors of your website who use Internet Explorer 6 will not have any difficulties viewing your pages. This restriction is valid only for you as the webmaster of the website.

FTP browser

You will need FTP access to your website. This kind of access is available on almost every web hosting. With the FTP connection data (see the previous table), you can connect to the hosting and upload all files that are required for installing and running CMS Made Simple.

There are many free FTP browsers that you can use. If you do not have an FTP browser, then I recommend the open source software **FileZilla** that is distributed free of charge on `http://filezilla-project.org/`. Download and install FileZilla right now.

 You need only **FileZilla Client**, not FileZilla Server!

File archiver

A file archiver is a program that you can use to extract the files of CMS Made Simple onto your local disk. As the files of CMS Made Simple are distributed as archives, the program should be able to handle `tar.gz` files. If you do not have a file archiver, then you can use the open source application **7-Zip** that can be freely downloaded from `http://www.7-zip.org`.

Now that we have all the access information and required software, we can start with the installation.

Uploading CMS Made Simple's files

The CMS Made Simple files can be downloaded from the official website of CMS Made Simple. Open `http://cmsmadesimple.org`, and click on **Downloads** in the top main navigation. You will see the list of files that are available for download, but you do not need all of them.

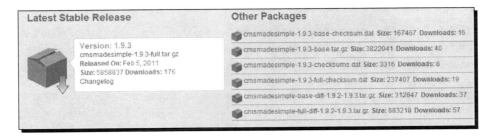

For every release, there is a bunch of files. There are two different versions of CMS Made Simple—**full version** and **base version**. There is no difference in the functionality or features, just in the included languages. The base version includes only English for the administration console of CMS Made Simple, whereas the full version includes all translations of the admin console (over twenty languages). So, when you need only the English language in the administration console of your website, you can take the base version. It is a bit smaller than the full version.

Find the file named `cmsmadesimple-X.X.X-full.tar.gz` or `cmsmadesimple-X.X.X-base.tar.gz` (depending on the version you need). Here, `X.X.X` stands for the number of the release. For example, for release 1.9.3 (displayed in the last screenshot), you will have to download the file `cmsmadesimple-1.9.3-full.tar.gz` or `cmsmadesimple-1.9.3-base.tar.gz`.

Click on the file to save it to your local disk. Then, using 7-Zip or any other file archiver of your choice, extract it onto your local disk, so that you can see what is inside. To extract using 7-Zip, right-click on the file, and select **7-Zip | Extract Here**, as shown in the following screenshot:

This will create a new file called `cmsmadesimple.1.9.3-full.tar`. The numbers in the filename depends on the version and release number of CMS Made Simple that you have downloaded. Right-click on this new file again, and select **7-Zip | Extract to "cmsmadesimple-1.9.3-full\"**, as shown in the next screenshot:

This action will create a new folder called `cmsmadesimple-1.9.3-full` on your local disk (or similar depending on the version and release number). This folder contains all files that you need to install CMS Made Simple. You have to upload them to your web space now.

Open FileZilla or an FTP browser of your choice. You have to connect to your web hosting to upload the files. In FileZilla, click on **File | Site Manager**. In **Site Manager**, click on the **New Site** button. You should see a dialog window, as shown in the following screenshot:

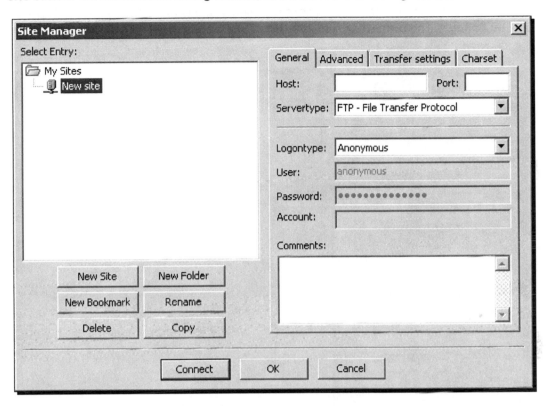

Enter your FTP host in the field **Host** on the right-hand side. Then click on the field **Logontype** and select **Normal** from the list. Now, you can enter your FTP **User** and FTP **Password** in the respective fields below. Your FTP login details should have been provided by your hosting company. Contact your hosting company's support if you encounter any issues. Click on **Connect**. The connection should be established, and you will see a screen similar to the following:

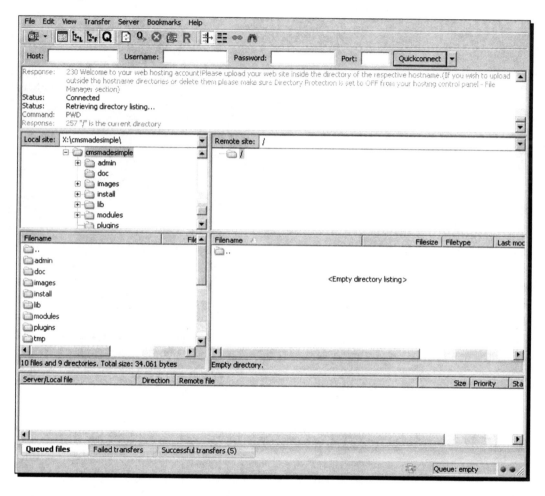

On the left-hand side of the screen, you can see your local disk. Navigate to the folder where you have extracted the installation files of CMS Made Simple. On the right-hand side, you see the remote folder of your web hosting.

You have to upload all files and folders from the local disk with exactly the same folder structure to the root or to a subdirectory on the web space. Your root directory can be public_html (or wwwroot or htdocs), please ask your provider if you are not sure where to upload the files. Locating the files in the root directory will make your site available to the users at http://www.yourdomain.com. If you create a subdirectory below the root directory, for example, public_html/somename, then your website will be available only in the subdirectory as http://www.yourdomain.com/somename. I recommend uploading the files to the root directory, unless you have already installed other applications there.

To upload all folders and files of CMS Made Simple, select everything on the left-hand (local) side, right-click, and select **Upload**.

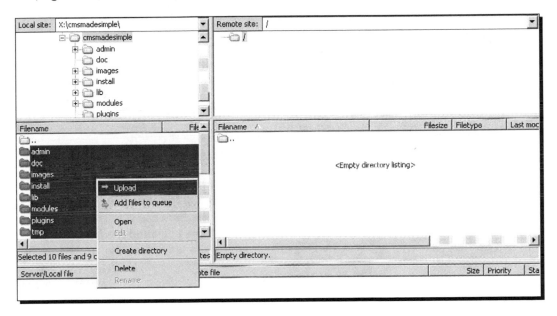

Depending on your connection, it may take more than fifteen minutes to upload the files. As the FTP browser creates some connections to the server, it may happen that some files are already being copied with other connections. In this case, you will see a window similar to the following:

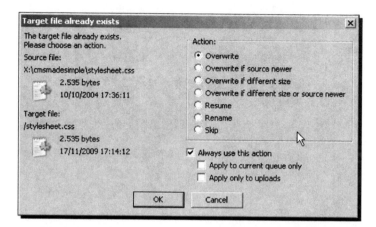

Choose **Overwrite** as the action, and check the box **Always use this action**. Wait until all the files have been transferred to the web space and until the upload is complete.

When the transfer is complete, you can start with the step-by-step installation program of CMS Made Simple. You start the installation process for CMS Made Simple in the browser by typing `http://www.yourdomain.com` in the address bar (you use your own domain name). If you do not see any installation screen, then you have uploaded the files into the wrong folder on your web space. Ask your provider where the files should be located.

Summary

In this chapter, a brief introduction to the entire book has been made.

Specifically, we covered the following:

- CMSes in general and the advantages of CMS Made Simple
- Preparing our system for installing CMSMS.

We're now ready to start with the installation of CMS Made Simple.

2
Getting Started

Before you start creating a website with CMS Made Simple, you have to install the application on your web hosting and make some important configurations that will have an impact on everything you do with the website in future. To install CMS Made Simple, you should understand what is web hosting. You should be able to create an empty database in your web hosting account and upload CMS Made Simple's installation files through FTP.

In this chapter, we will:

- Install CMS Made Simple
- Learn about the admin console and how it is organized
- Finish the installation
- Configure the e-mail settings

CMS Made Simple is a PHP application that uses a MySQL database. This means that you need web hosting with PHP and MySQL to run CMS Made Simple. You can install a web server on a local PC for testing environments and/or on remote web hosting for live websites. The requirements for CMS Made Simple are as follows:

- Web server on Linux/Unix or Windows 2000/XP/ME/2003 or OS X
- PHP 5.2.4+ (recommended 5.2.12+)
  - `safe_mode` should be off
  - At least 16 MB of available memory for PHP
  - PHP tokenizer support enabled
  - At least one of ImageMagick or GDlib enabled
- MySQL 4.1+ or PostgreSQL 7+
- Enough access to your server to upload files and change some permissions

These requirements are not special and are covered by most hosting providers. To test CMS Made Simple for free without any obligation, you can even set up CMS Made Simple on free web hosting that meets the requirements stated. If in doubt, ask on the CMS Made Simple forum (`http://forum.cmsmadesimple.org`) for any hosting recommendations.

Installing CMS Made Simple step-by-step

The CMS Made Simple installer is started automatically when you enter your domain name in the address bar of the browser. The installer assists you step-by-step during the entire installation process.

Choosing a language

First you choose the installation language. In the drop-down field, you see all languages available in the installation package. In the base version of CMS Made Simple, you can choose only English. The full version has more languages included.

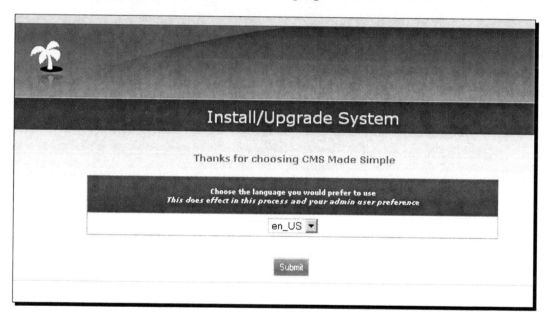

Consider that the language you choose here is used only during the installation. The language of the website and admin console can be changed later on. Click on **Submit**.

Step 1: Validating file integrity (optional)

In the first step, you can optionally validate the integrity of the installation file. This will help you identify potential problems, for example if some files have been damaged during FTP transfer or are incomplete due to network issues. If there were no issues while uploading the files to the web hosting, then ignore this step and click on **Continue**. Validation can also be done any time after the installation is complete.

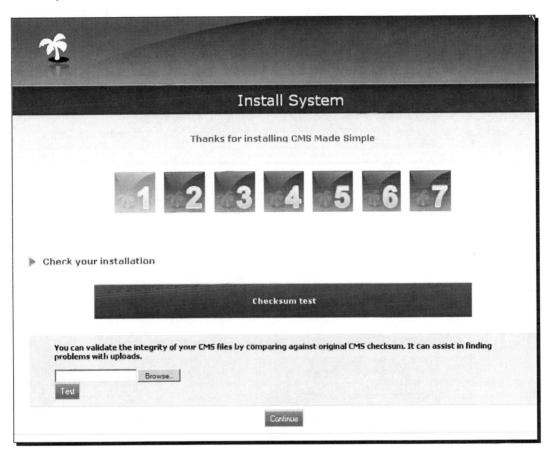

If you would like to validate, then you will need the checksum file corresponding to your version: cmsmadesimple-1.9.3-full-checksum.dat or cmsmadesimple-1.9.3-base-checksum.dat. This file is available for download from the official website. Go to http://cmsmadesimple.org, click **Downloads**, and save the checksum file to your local disk. Choose the file in the field above, and click on **Test**.

This step is optional. Click on **Continue**.

Step 2: Checking requirements

In the second step, the installation program tests the settings of your web hosting. Check the **Result** column in the **Required settings** section. There should not be any failures or warnings.

The most common failure is:

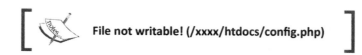

File not writable! (/xxxx/htdocs/config.php)

Required settings	
Test	**Result**
Checking for PHP version 5.2.4+ (minimum 5.2.4, recommend 5.2.12 or greater) You have 5.2.6 *CMS Made Simple requires a php version of 5.2.4 or greater (you have 5.2.6), but PHP 5.2.12 or greater is recommended to ensure maximum compatibility with third party addons*	❗
Checking for md5 Function You have On	✔
Checking for GD library You have 2	✔
Checking write permission on config.php	✔
Checking for tempnam Function You have On	✔
Magic quotes in runtime You have Off	✔
DB drivers You have mysqli,mysql	✔
Checking if the httpd process can create a file inside of a directory it created.	✔
Testing error_reporting to ensure E_STRICT is disabled	✔

This means that the file `config.php` either does not exist in the root directory of the installation or there is no write permission for it.

If the file does not exist, create an empty file named `config.php` in a text editor (not a word processor). In Windows, open Notepad (this text editor comes with Windows), and without typing anything in the document, click on **File | Save As**. Choose a location to save the file, and use `config.php` (including the quotes) as the filename to ensure that the right extension (`.php`) is used. Upload that file via FTP to the folder where the CMS Made Simple installation files were uploaded. The `config.php` file should be in the same folder as the `index.php` file, as shown in the following screenshot:

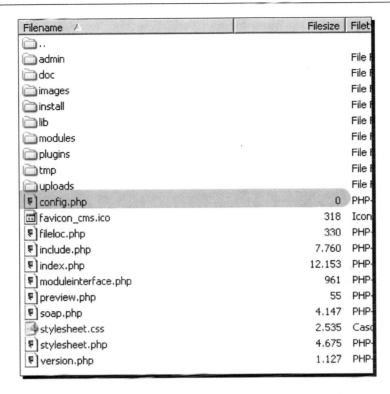

Check if the file you have created and uploaded has the file type PHP (some editors may append `.txt` extension to the end of the filename). If necessary, rename the file to `config.php`.

If the file already exists, open FileZilla or any other browser of your choice and right-click on it. Choose **File permissions** and enter *777* in the **Numeric value** field. Click on **OK**.

Go back to your browser, and click on **Try again** at the end of the settings check; the failure should disappear.

If you have other failures or warnings in the **Required settings** section and if you're unsure how to handle them, then take a screenshot of the page, and send it to your provider. He/she will help you to solve the problem.

You can ignore warnings in the **Recommended settings** section. You most probably will not encounter any problems while running your website even if you do not correct them. However, if you can follow the recommendations given to resolve the warnings, then please do it.

Recommended settings		
Test		**Result**
Checking PHP memory limit (minimum 16M, recommend 24M or greater)	You have 300M	✓
Checking PHP time limit in second (minimum 30, recommend 60 or greater)	You have 60	✓
Checking PHP register globals	You have Off	✓
Checking output buffering	You have 4096	✓
Checking PHP disable functions		✓
Checking for safe mode	You have Off	✓
Check for PHP Open Basedir		✓
Test for remote URL ✓ fsockopen: Connection ok! ✓ fopen: Connection ok!		✓
Checking file uploads	You have On	✓
Checking max post size (minimum 2M, recommend 10M or greater)	You have 10M	✓
Checking max upload file size (minimum 2M, recommend 10M or greater)	You have 10M	✓
Checking if /httpdocs/uploads is writable	You have /httpdocs/uploads	✓
Checking if /httpdocs/uploads/images is writable	You have /httpdocs/uploads/images	✓
Checking if /httpdocs/modules is writable	You have /httpdocs/modules	✓
Checking if session.save_path is writable	You have c:/wamp/tmp	✓
session.use_cookies	You have On	✓
Checking for basic XML (expat) support	You have On	✓
Checking for file_get_contents	You have On	✓
Checking if ini_set works	You have On	✓

On some web servers, you have to change permissions of the uploaded folders. If you're using FileZilla, then right-click on the remote folder, and select **File permissions**. In the dialog window **Change file attributes**, enter **777** in the **Numeric value** field. You should make those changes to the following folders:

- ◆ tmp/templates_c
- ◆ tmp/cache

- uploads
- uploads/images
- modules

Click on **Continue**.

Step 3: Testing file creation mask (optional)

In this step, you can optionally test if CMS Made Simple is allowed to create files on your web hosting. Click on **Test** or just ignore this step and click on **Continue**.

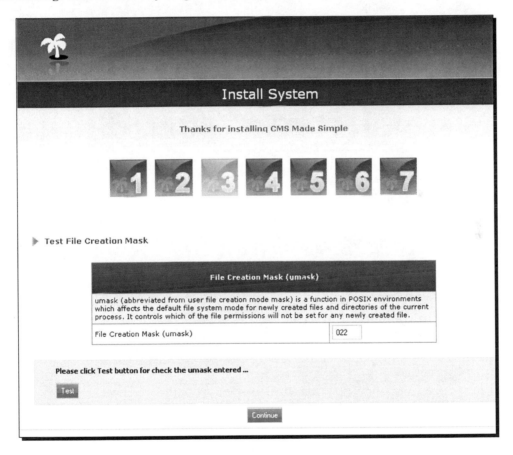

Step 4: Admin account information

Pay attention to this step. You are going to create an administrator account for your website. With this data, you gain access to the administration console of your website after it has been installed. Remember or write down the administrator's username and password that you enter in this step. Provide a valid e-mail address for your account. If you forget your password someday, then a reminder will be sent to this e-mail address.

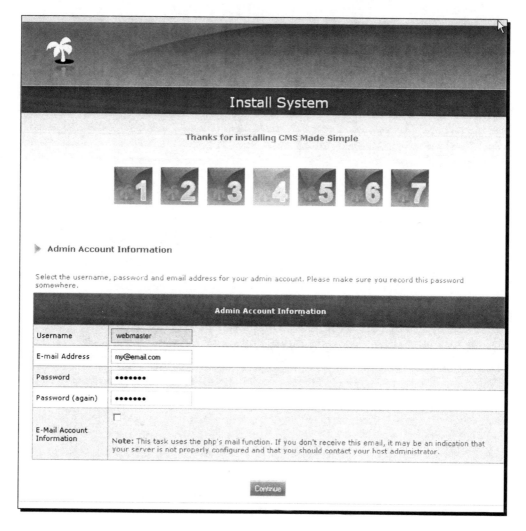

You can check the box for **E-Mail Account Information**. CMS Made Simple will try to send a confirmation mail to your e-mail account. However, do not rely on it due to the individual hosting settings. We will configure the e-mail settings of CMS Made Simple later in this chapter.

Click on **Continue**.

Step 5: Database information

In this step, change the name of the website or leave it as it is. This information can be changed any time after the installation.

For the database information, use the access data for the database that you gained while preparing for the installation.

1. Replace **Database host address** with your individual data.
2. Replace **Database name** with the name of your database.
3. Enter the database **Username**.
4. Enter the database **Password** and optionally the **Database port** (if any).

These are the access credentials for your database. If you are not sure what to enter in these fields, then ask your hosting provider.

Sample content and templates

In the last field of this installation step, you have to decide whether you would like to install sample content and templates. Sample content is a useful resource for your first introduction to CMS Made Simple, as it includes more than twenty pages with an overview of what CMS Made Simple is and how it works.

Click on **Continue**.

Step 6: Creating tables

If the connection to the database was successful and the tables in the database were created, then you will see the message **Success!** at the end of this step, as shown in the next screenshot. Leave all the values in the fields below the message as they are, and click on **Continue**.

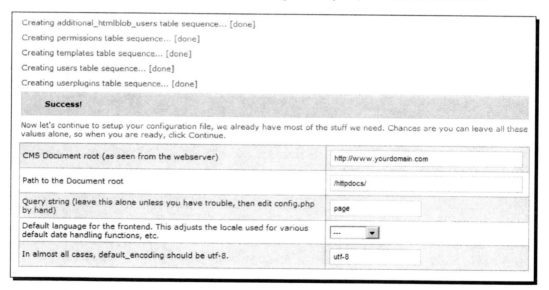

Step 7: Installation is complete

You're done! Congratulations. You can access your website by typing the domain name in the address bar of the browser, for example, `http://www.yourdomain.com`. The admin console is placed at `http://www.yourdomain.com/admin`. Click on **go to the Admin Panel**. Normally, you are already logged in to it. If not, then use the data that you entered in step 4 of the installation process.

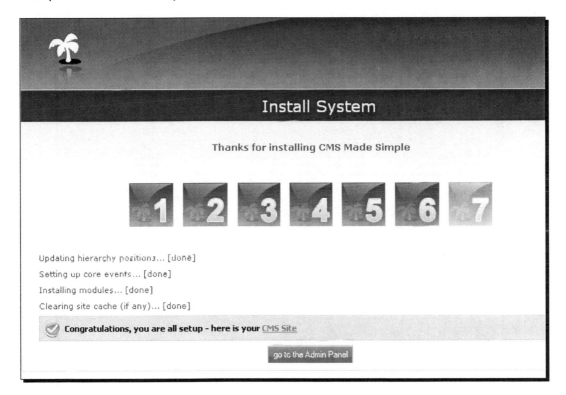

Understanding the admin console

The admin console is the heart of CMS Made Simple. This is where the website administrator (you) will work from. Here you add pages and fill them with content, choose the layout and style of your pages, install extensions for extra functionality, set permissions for users and groups, and configure the entire website.

 The admin console is the backend; as opposed to the frontend, which is what visitors to your site can see.

Log in to the admin console with the address `http://www.yourdomain.com/admin`, using the data from step 4 of the installation process. The administrator of the website can also add additional users.

Everything in the admin console is accessed through the main horizontal menu. When you first enter the admin area, you also see a sitemap of what can be accessed through each menu.

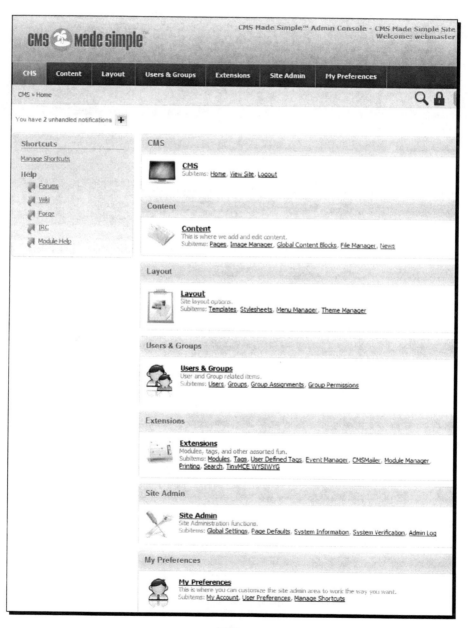

In the sitemap for any menu item, when you click on the main horizontal menu (**CMS**, **Content**, **Layout**, **Users & Groups**, and so on), all subitems of that menu item are shown.

Let's take a quick walkthrough of what's in the admin console.

- ◆ **CMS**: In the **CMS** menu, you can open the admin sitemap (see the next screenshot), the frontend page (**View Site**) in a new window, or **Logout**.

CMS
Subitems: Home, View Site, Logout

- ◆ **Content**: Here you can manage the content of your site. You can add and edit pages, upload and manage images and files, and also add, edit, and remove news. If you have installed additional content modules (such as a guestbook or FAQ), then they appear in this section as well. Lastly, in the content menu, you can create global content blocks that will be used on the entire website in different places and edited from one place.

Content
This is where we add and edit content.
Subitems: Pages, Image Manager, Global Content Blocks, File Manager, News

- ◆ **Layout**: Here you can style and format the look of your page in the way you want. For the general layout, you use templates. In the layout menu, you can also access the **Stylesheets**. Using stylesheets (CSS), you can style different elements of your page.

Layout
Site layout options.
Subitems: Templates, Stylesheets, Menu Manager, Theme Manager

- **Users & Groups**: With this menu item, you can add users that should have access to the admin console of your website and select what permissions they will have. You can put users in groups to easily select permissions for the whole group at the same time.

Users & Groups
User and Group related items.
Subitems: Users, Groups, Group Assignments, Group Permissions

- **Extensions**: These are add-ons that give extra functionality to CMS Made Simple. The standard installation of CMS Made Simple includes only some basic features. With extensions, you can add more or less any functionality to your site. Extensions can be either modules or tags (also called plugins).

Extensions
Modules, tags, and other assorted fun.
Subitems: Modules, Tags, User Defined Tags, Event Manager, CMSMailer, Module Manager, Printing, Search, TinyMCE WYSIWYG

- **Site Admin**: Here you can change the settings and preferences for the entire website, get system information, and verify the file's integrity. Any changes made to your website by you or other users are tracked in **Admin Log**.

Site Admin
Site Administration functions.
Subitems: Global Settings, Page Defaults, System Information, System Verification, Admin Log

- **My Preferences**: Here you can change your personal settings. You can also manage shortcuts to the pages that are most frequently used in the admin area. Click on **My Account**, if you would like to change the username of the administrator account, his/her password, or the e-mail associated with the account.

My Preferences
This is where you can customize the site admin area to work the way you want.
Subitems: My Account, User Preferences, Manage Shortcuts

Finishing the installation

Immediately after installation, you see two unhandled notifications in the dashboard area below the main menu. Click on the sign **+** beside the notifications to expand the dashboard area.

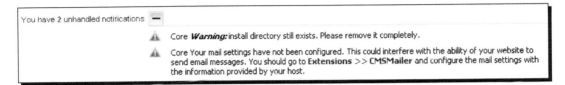

The first notification informs you that the install folder still exists on the web server. This folder contains the installation program you have used to set up CMS Made Simple. Once CMS Made Simple is installed and is running, you don't need this folder, and therefore, you should delete it or at least rename it. If you do not, then everybody can start the installation program again and thus replace your website with a new installation. This would be a big security issue, so delete the folder right now.

After the folder is deleted (or renamed), refresh the admin console to see the first message disappear.

The second message deals with the e-mail settings you should configure before running CMS Made Simple.

Sending e-mails with CMS

CMS Made Simple sends e-mails with the module **CMSMailer**. The configuration of the **CMSMailer** module is very important. If you do not configure it, then you will not receive the e-mail with new login information, should you ever forget your administrator password. This module is also used by many other CMS Made Simple modules that send out e-mails such as **FrontEndUsers**, **Orders**, or **FormBuilder**.

You will see this notification in the dashboard of CMS Made Simple till you have configured the module.

In the admin console, in the main horizontal navigation, select **Extensions | CMSMailer**. Set the **Character Set** to **utf-8**. Then, choose **sendmail** in the **Mailer method** field. Fill the field **From address** with an existing e-mail address. When CMS sends e-mails, the recipient will see this e-mail as the sender address. You have to enter an existing e-mail address here, as due to spam and security settings on your web hosting, CMS Made Simple will probably not be able to send out e-mails.

Fill in the **From Username** field. The name given here will be assigned to the mail address in the recipient's mail client.

Character Set:

utf-8

Mailer method:

sendmail ▾

Mail method to use (sendmail, smtp, mail). Usually smtp is the most reliable.

SMTP host name
(or IP address):

localhost

SMTP hostname (only valid for the smtp mailer method)

Port of SMTP server:

25

SMTP port number (usually 25) (only valid for the smtp mailer method)

From address:

something@yourdomain.com

Address used as the sender in all emails.
Note, this email address must be set correctly for your host or you will have difficulty sending emails.
If you do not know the proper value for this setting, you may need to contact your host.

From Username:

Me

Friendly name used for sending all emails

Sendmail location:

/usr/sbin/sendmail

The complete path to your sendmail executable (only valid for the sendmail mailer method)

SMTP timeout:

1000

The number of seconds in an SMTP conversation before an error occurs (valid for the smtp mailer method)

SMTP Authentication:

☐

Does your smtp host require authentication (valid only for the smtp mailer method)

Username:

SMTP authentication username (valid only for smtp mailer method, when smtp auth is selected)

Password:

SMTP authentication password (valid only for smtp mailer method, when smtp auth is selected)

Submit   Cancel

Test Email Address:

Send Test Message

Click on **Submit**, and confirm the changes.

Test your settings using the last field on the same page. In the **Test Email Address** field, enter any e-mail address (not one from the field **From Address**) where you have access to the mail box. CMS Made Simple will send a test message to the e-mail address given in this field. Click on the **Send Test Message** button, and control the incoming messages of the e-mail address given in the field **Test Email Address**. Did you receive the test message?

If not, wait for some time and then check your spam folder. Sometimes test messages are filtered out and treated as spam. If the test message has not been sent, then something is wrong with the configuration of the **CMSMailer** module.

Known issues

- ◆ Check the **Sendmail location** field (your hosting provider has to confirm that it is right or he/she should provide you with your individual location).
- ◆ Check the e-mail address entered in the **From address** field. It must be an existing e-mail address, and it has to be located on your web hosting. If you enter any other e-mail address, then your server will not be able to send out e-mails. To use e-mail addresses of the public e-mail services such as Gmail or GMX, you have to configure the module with SMTP as the **Mailer method**. This method requires that you fill in the fields considering SMTP. SMTP settings are individual for any e-mail provider.
- ◆ Check the spam folder and filter of the **Test Email Address**, sometimes test messages are sorted out or immediately deleted.

Summary

At the end of this chapter, you should have a clean installation of CMS Made Simple.

Specifically, we covered:

- ◆ Installation of the program: CMS Made Simple is delivered with a simple installation program that guides you step-by-step through the setup process. We have performed the steps to get CMS Made Simple running.
- ◆ Overview of the admin console: The admin console is like a cockpit in a plane. It is a place from where you can control the entire website. In the course of this book, you will learn every part in more detail.
- ◆ Sending e-mails: You have configured CMS Made Simple so that it can send mails from the admin console. If you forget your admin password, then you will receive a reminder e-mail with instructions on how to recover it. All core and most of the third-party modules of CMS Made Simple rely on this functionality. Once configured, you do not need to make it for each module separately.

In the next chapter, we will see how you create the website structure and build website navigation.

3

Creating Pages and Navigation

In this chapter, you will learn how to create new pages, edit existing pages, control the navigation of your website, and organize pages according to your website's plan. As a result, you will get a complete website structure, a kind of skeleton for your website.

Let's see how we can plan a website. Yes, we should plan before making anything material. You have to spend time on this step because you will in fact save time afterwards by avoiding the need to do some time-consuming rebuilding, recreating, or reorganizing of your website.

Take a piece of paper and write down the main parts of the website and its purpose. Write down the main idea of the website, then add the main parts (building your navigation structure) and proceed until you do not have any other ideas. Do not try to find any solution or the right tool to create your website at this time. Do not ask: "How would I realize this or that?". You have to hold everything you would like to see on the website without considering the technical details. Plan as if you have a magic wand for creating websites.

For example, a company website needs a section where the company is represented, a way to display its products or services catalog, a client center, and a contact form; refine and add each part.

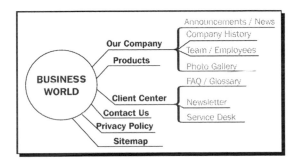

Planning your website will also help us to choose the appropriate design for it. The best design will fail if your website plan does not match the already created navigation. In the example website plan, you can easily indicate the main navigation (marked in bold), subnavigation (marked in grey), and the common structure of the website. It is important to have a rough plan and that we do not change it very often.

It is likely that you will have more and more ideas while planning the website—write them down! The advantage of planning in this way is that you are not restricted at all. You can note down all your ideas now, select the feasible tasks, and concentrate on them. Later on, you can add new parts that are not mandatory for the first implementation of your website. It is important to differentiate between nice-to-have features and something that you cannot live without.

If you create a website plan to keep all your ideas in mind, you can avoid creating pages that contain only one sentence like "Under construction". Good websites don't have any pages that are not ready. If there are any, then they should not be shown to the visitor. Imagine seeing a notice about personal style consultation in the window of a clothes shop. You go into the shop, but the clerk says: "Sorry! This service is still under construction." What was the purpose of calling attention to it? Some webmasters add such pages to the website just "to keep them in mind". You can keep them in mind in a more efficient way if you write down the main structure of your website in a separate place.

Ask your friends or family members what they plan to add to the website and keep their ideas as well. Consider different age groups and interests while planning to broaden the scope of your visitors.

If everything is perfect, then go through the main sections in your website plan and mark the parts that can be done immediately (all the sections on the previously mentioned website plan will be discussed in this guide). Other parts should not be deleted from the plan but marked as postponed. Normally, you have enough stuff at the beginning. Concentrate on these feasible points and keep the postponed points in mind.

When you are ready with the website plan, print it out, put it beside your PC, and start working on your website.

In this chapter, we will:

- Create and edit some pages
- Learn about page hierarchy
- Control the navigation of the website

Creating pages

We will begin by creating a rough structure for our website. A website consists of pages, which are linked to each other. The navigation of the website helps the visitor to find the pages containing the requested information. A website must have at least one page and therefore, the first page is already created in your admin console after installation. It is the start page of your website, and it is called **Home**.

Time for action – adding a new page to the website

Your website requires a page where information about the company is represented. It is the page for the section **Our Company** in the website plan. Let's create a new page as follows:

1. In the admin console of your website, click on **Content | Pages** and then on the link **Add New Content**.

2. Fill in the field's **Title** and **Content Type** as shown in the following screenshot:

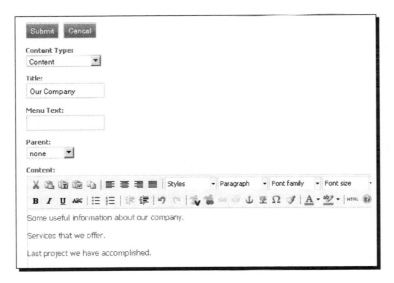

3. Click on **Submit**.

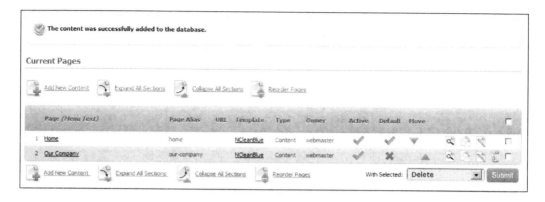

4. Click on the magnifying glass icon at the top-right of the admin console to view your website and find the new page added to the main navigation of the website.

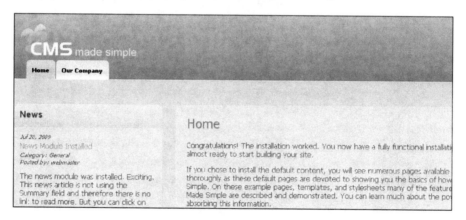

What just happened?

You have just added a new page to your website. The page has the title **Our Company** and is now listed in current pages of your website in the admin console. The page is also automatically added to the main navigation of the website. It has sample company information in the content field. This text is displayed on the **Our Company** page on the website when you navigate to the page.

You have entered only a little information to create a new page. However, other things happened.

Menu text has been created from the title of the page. A page address (URL) has been created from the title of the page. It is a part of the page link that is placed after `index.php?page=` in the address bar of the browser when you navigate to the page. In CMS Made Simple, we call this part the **page alias**. The page alias is unique within your website. You can have a lot of pages with the same title and menu text, but all these pages will have a different page alias. As the page alias is used to create a link to a specific page, you cannot have two different pages with the same link, and logically you cannot have the same page alias for two different pages.

You do not need to care about integrating the created page into the navigation of your website. All created pages will be displayed in the navigation if you do not state anything else.

Now, you can create all pages from the first level of your website, thus creating the main navigation on the top of the website. Add the following pages:

- **Products**
- **Client Center**
- **Contact Us**
- **Privacy Policy**
- **Sitemap**

Control the list of current pages in the admin console and on your website.

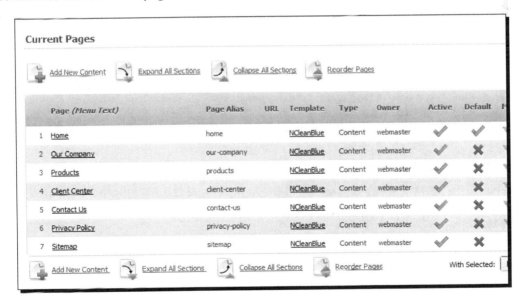

Editing pages

All pages can be edited at any time from the list of pages in the admin console.

Time for action – editing existing pages

We do not like the menu text for the page **Home** and would like to change it to **Start**. We would also like to replace the title and text on the page. In the admin console, open **Content | Pages**, and click on the **Home** page.

> **1.** Make changes to the **Home** page, as shown in the following screenshot:

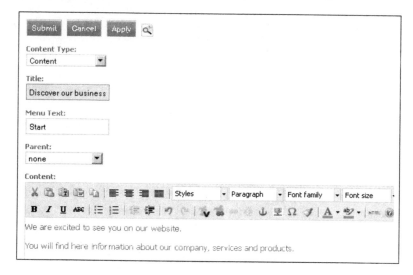

> **2.** Click the **Apply** button to update the page.
>
> **3.** Click the magnifier icon beside the **Apply** button to view the changes on the website.

What just happened?

You have changed the menu text shown in the navigation of the website. You have also replaced text on the page. At the end, you applied the changes and viewed the page in a new window.

You used the **Submit** button to save the changes and close the page in one step. The **Apply** button does not close the page. Applying changes allows you to edit the page without closing it, and thus avoid needing to reopen it for editing after each change. The **Apply** button appears only if you edit an existing page. It is not available when you are creating a new page.

Use the **Apply** button frequently, especially if you are working with large amounts of text, keep a copy of it in a separate editor window. If the connection is lost or time's out, then the page will fail to load in the browser and the modifications would be lost.

Previewing changes

If you would like to preview the changes before saving, switch to the **Preview** tab without applying the changes. You can see the changes displayed in the preview window, but they will not be visible to the visitors of your website at this moment. Once you have applied or submitted the edited page, the changes will be made visible to your site's visitors.

Changing the page alias

You can change the page alias of the page as well. Switch to the **Options** tab while editing the page, and enter the desired alias in the **Page Alias** field. Think of page alias as the link to the page. You are not allowed to enter special characters in this field, so use spaces or leave it empty. Choose the name entered here carefully as you will not be able to change it easily after your website is published online. Once your website is discovered by the search engines, the pages will be displayed in the search results with links made from the page alias. If you change the page alias, then the page will not be found and your visitors will see an error message instead of the desired information.

Deleting pages

You can delete your pages from the list of current pages in the admin console (**Content | Pages**). Find the page you do not need anymore, and click on the dust bin icon for that page. Be careful! Deleted pages cannot be restored. If you would like to keep the page for personal purposes only, then make it inactive (see the section titled *Control the navigation of the website* for more information).

Formatting page content

You have already created some pages and edited them. Notice that the text you have entered in the **Content** field appears on the website in a certain place. The text is only a fraction of the entire page. You cannot change the design of the navigation, the header, or the footer part from here.

If you were just an editor of the website (not a designer and not an administrator), then you would create or edit your articles here, but would not have the ability to change anything else on the website. This is the most important principle of a **content management system (CMS)**. We separate design from content to separate different tasks that can be accomplished by different persons. It also helps to separate the content of the layout and design so that it allows for globally changing the appearance of the website without going through all the circles of hell.

An editor needs to have the ability to format his writing by making some phrases bold and creating lists or link to other pages of the website. Normally, HTML knowledge is required for this, unless you use the **WYSIWYG editor**.

WYSIWYG means **What You See Is What You Get** and gives you the ability to format the text of a page with a common word processing feature. Additionally, the text is displayed in the editor in the same way that it will appear on the website.

Working with the WYSIWYG editor does not require any HTML knowledge to create, edit, and format the text part of your website.

The WYSIWYG editor is the central and most important feature of every CMS. If you create a website with CMS, then you are going to consequently add content to your website. It means that apart from other modules, the WYSIWYG editor will be one of the most frequently used features of your CMS. Therefore, it is important to understand how the editor can help you and what you can do to make it suit your needs. There are some WYSIWYG editors available, for CMS Made Simple, the editor called **TinyMCE** is the most well integrated one.

In the admin console, go to **Content | Pages** and select any page for editing. The **Content** field uses a WYSIWYG editor (you can see a toolbar above the content field), which is shown in the following screenshot:

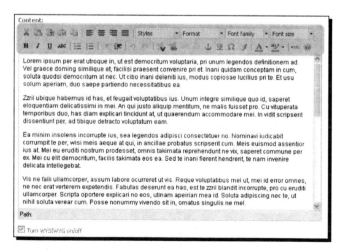

The toolbar of the editor is self-explanatory and is similar to most popular word processing programs. There are many more settings that can simplify your life if you discover them.

Often, a large amount of text is written in word processing programs like Microsoft Word. If you copy the text from Word directly into the content of the field, then it will cause a lot of problems because of the bad HTML produced by Word. In the toolbar of the editor, there is a special button (the fourth in the first line) to paste text from Word. Always use this button to copy text from Word as it will filter any messy code from your text.

Configuring TinyMCE

In the admin console, click on **Extensions | TinyMCE WYSIWYG**. You can change the width and height of the editor field here. By default, the size of the editor field is set automatically; change it according to your screen preference to gain more space to write and read.

Deselect the **Auto** field, enter the desired width and height, and click on **Save settings**. There is a tab "Testing area" where you can immediately see the changes. This field allows you to preview changes so that you do not need to edit pages to control the appearance of the editor.

On the **Profiles** tab, you can add even more features. For the administrator of the website, the changes have to be made in the **Advanced backend profile settings** section. Select the **Allow table operations** field to be able to create and edit tables with the WYSIWYG editor. After saving the profile, you will find the third line in the toolbar of the editor that helps to build HTML tables.

Check the **Show file management options** field if you would like to upload images directly from the editor. Click on Save profile, switch to the tab Testing area, and then click on the **Insert/edit image** icon in the toolbar. A small window pops up where you can change an image URL. Click on it, and the content of your images folder is displayed, as shown in the next screenshot. Normally, no uploads are allowed from this window. However, as you have activated the file management option, you will find the **File operations** section above the image list where you can upload your images.

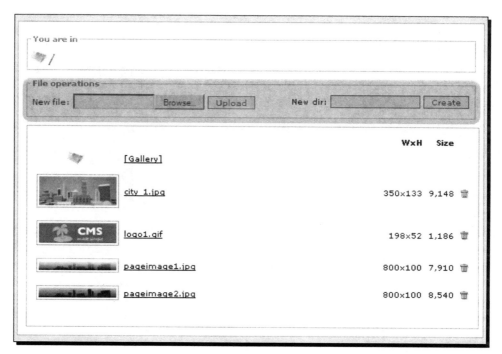

Use folders to organize the images from the very beginning, or else you will end up with hundreds of assorted images in no time, and it will be a big problem to rearrange them, as they are already linked from various pages. Having a lot of images in one folder will slow down the loading of the file picker and finding the image you are looking for will become a challenging task.

Continue to customize the editor in the **Plugins** tab. There are some useful plugins that are not active by default, but can be activated if needed. I recommend activating the following plugins:

- **print**: Allows you to print the text from the editor
- **fullscreen**: Adds a fullscreen editing mode
- **searchreplace**: Adds search/replace dialogs for the text

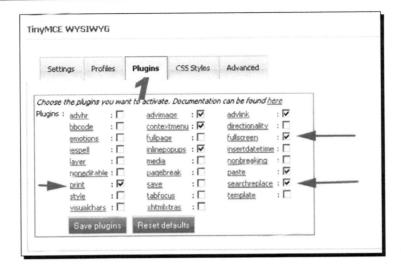

Click on **Save plugins**. Only the icon for fullscreen is added to the second toolbar before the help icon. The other two do not appear. Why? Let's take a step back and check the **Profiles** tab again. In the **Advanced backend profile settings** section, you can see three toolbar lines. These lines control the order of the icons shown in the editor in the first, second, and third (yet empty) line. The single buttons are represented with their names in the toolbar fields, as shown in the following screenshot:

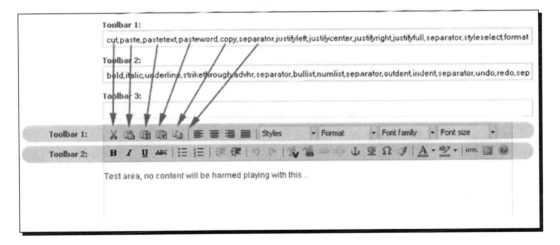

You can delete some of them, change the order, or add new ones. That is what we are going to do.

Time for action – activating search and replace function

There is a useful plugin that can search the entire contents of a page and replace all instances of a word or phrase with something different. Let's see how we can activate this plugin in TinyMCE.

1. In the admin console, click on **Extensions | TinyMCE WYSIWYG**.

2. Click the **Plugins** tab.

3. Select the checkbox beside the plugin called **searchreplace**, as shown in the following screenshot:

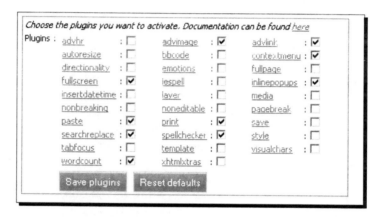

4. Click the **Save plugins** button.

5. Switch to the **Profiles** tab.

6. In the **Advanced backend profile settings** section, add the words **search, replace** to the **Toolbar 3** field, as shown in the following screenshot:

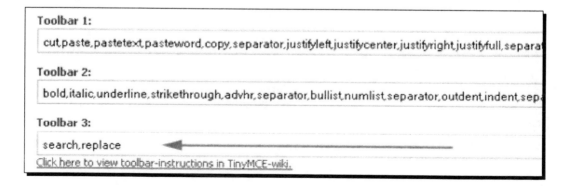

7. Click on the **Save profile** button, and see the additional functions added to the third line of the toolbar, as shown in the following screenshot:

What just happened?

Firstly, you activated the plugin in the **Plugins** tab. Activating a plugin means that the plugin is loaded with TinyMCE. But it is not enough to just activate it. In the second step, you had to customize the toolbar of TinyMCE to inform the editor where the buttons for the plugin should be shown.

You saw that a single plugin can provide two buttons. Therefore, there were two words you had to enter in the field **Toolbar 3**. The first one, **search**, was for the search button, and the second one, **replace**, was for the replace function. They must not be used together. You can omit the first or the second one if you do not need that specific functionality.

> Add the plugin removeformat in the **Toolbar 3** field. This is a plugin that must not be activated first as it belongs to standard. The plugin allows the removal of any formatting from the text without looking at the HTML.

There are more advanced settings in the WYSIWYG editor. To understand them, you need to know how CMS Made Simple works in general. I recommend referring to the settings of the WYSIWYG editor again and again while reading this book to make working with the editor more efficient.

Adding meta tags

Meta tags contain additional information about your website. This information is not directly displayed to the visitors of the website; as the purpose of meta tags is to supply additional information about your website to search engines and web browsers. We have to distinguish between meta tags that are the same on each page of your website and tags that are unique to a specific page of your content.

Meta elements are HTML or XHTML elements that provide additional information for search engines. They are not visible to the visitors of the website. Such elements must be placed as tags in the head section of the page. Meta elements can be used to specify the page description, keywords, and any other metadata.

Meta element specifies name and the associated content describing the page. For example:

```
<meta name="keywords" content="business company,services" />
```

In this example, the meta tag identifies the page as containing keywords relevant to the phrase business company and the word services.

Time for action – adding meta tags to pages

Let's add some specific meta tags to the start page of our website.

1. In the admin console, open **Content | Pages**.

2. Click on the start page **Start** to edit it.

3. Switch to the **Options** tab.

4. In the field **Page Specific Metadata**, add meta tags that are specific to the page.

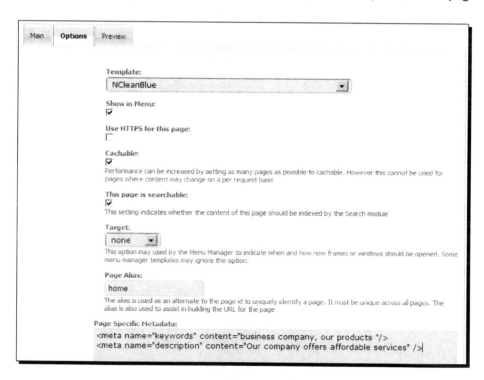

5. Click on **Apply** at the bottom of the page.

6. Click on the magnifier icon beside the **Apply** button.

7. See the head section of the website in the source code of the page.

What just happened?

You have added meta tags in plain HTML to the start page of your website. These meta tags appear only on this specific page. Generally, meta tags for the description and keywords should be different on each page.

 Any other tags (not only meta tags) for the head section of the generated page can be added here as well.

Adding global meta tags

Some global meta tags are already added to the standard installation of CMS Made Simple. You can see these meta tags in the source code of every page generated by CMS Made Simple:

```
<meta name="Generator" content="CMS Made Simple - Copyright (C) 2004-9
Ted Kulp. All rights reserved." />
<meta http-equiv="Content-Type" content="text/html; charset=utf-8" />
```

To change or delete the tags, click on **Site Admin | Global Settings** in the admin console. Find the meta tags listed above in the field **Global Metadata**. You can add your own meta tags in this field using plain HTML.

 Any other tags (not only meta tags) for the head section of all pages can be added here as well.

Understanding page hierarchy

All pages you have added in the last step are now displayed in the main navigation of your website and can be found in the current list of the pages in the admin console. But there are some more pages in our website plan that have to be added to the hierarchy.

With page hierarchy, you define the pages as being above, below, or at the same level as another page. If a page is not shown in the main navigation, then we call it a **subpage**. It also means that there is a parent page above the subpage.

Time for action – adding subpages to a website

Let's create four pages below the **Our Company** page according to the website plan.

1. In the admin console of your website, click on **Content | Pages** and then on the **Add New Content** link.

2. Fill the fields **Title** and **Content** as shown in the following screenshot and choose the page **2. -Our Company** from the drop-down field **Parent**.

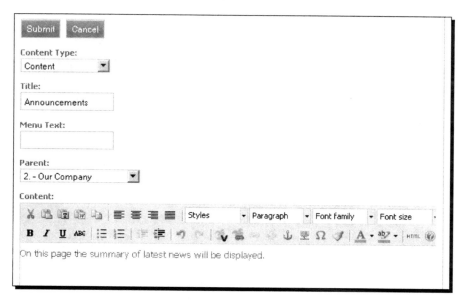

3. Click on **Submit**.

4. Click on the triangle to expand the list of pages below the page **Our Company** and to view the subpage created.

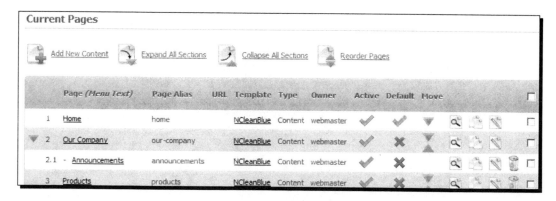

5. Click on the magnifying glass icon beside the just created page to view the page on the website.

What just happened?

You have added a new page. This time you have selected a parent page placing the new page in the hierarchy below the parent one. In the admin console, you can see that the page is now indented under the parent page. It gets the number **2.1**, saying that the page belongs to the page with number **2** and is its first child page. You will not find the page in the main navigation of the website, however, you can see the page added to the subnavigation, if you move your mouse over **Our Company** in the navigation.

We need the page hierarchy to organize our pages into main sections and to have the subnavigations built automatically.

If you would like to change the position of the page in the hierarchy, you have to edit the page by clicking on it in the page list. Select another parent page in the field **Parent** and save the changes. If you choose **none** in the drop-down list, then the page is moved to the first level and thus displayed in the main navigation.

Use the **Expand All Sections** link at the bottom of the list of current pages in order to show all hierarchy levels. With **Collapse All Sections**, you can hide all subpages and show only the first level.

You can reorder the pages that are on the same level by using icons from the **Move** column (down and up). However, if you have to move one or more pages from the very bottom to the top of the list, it can be hard to do it with move icons (especially if you have a large number of pages). Use the **Reorder pages** link in this case. This feature allows you to reorder pages by clicking on a page and dragging it to a different position within the same hierarchy level.

Reordering pages in the admin console will also change the order of appearance in the navigation of your website.

Breadcrumbs

Your hierarchy is also displayed in the so called breadcrumbs—navigation aid displayed on the website above the content. It starts with **You are here**, displays the trail of the page and provides links back to the parent page(s) of the current one.

Search engine friendly URLs

While creating your website, you probably thought about how you would promote it in search engines. Before you start to share the URLs of your website's pages, it is advisable to set up search engine friendly addresses.

Search engine friendly URLs do not contain any dynamic components in them and are more readable for visitors of your website and search engines. Compare the following two URLs:

```
http://yourdomain.com/index.php?page=products
```

```
http://yourdomain.com/products
```

Which page address is better? Search engines index your website better if your website uses the second version. Some pages with dynamic query strings in the address (as in the first example) are never indexed, and some of them will take longer to get into the search results.

If you do not care about search engines, then think about the visitors of the website. How easy is it to type or write down the address of the specific page if we do not use the second rewritten version? Imagine your visitor would like to recommend the page. He would do it without any difficulties with search engine friendly URLs and may fail with the first example.

However, after installing your website with CMS Made Simple, you will find that the URLs of your pages are built in the first way. You can easily change them to achieve better results with the website.

Time for action – creating search engine friendly URLs

To enable search engine friendly URLs on your website, perform the following steps:

1. Start FileZilla or any other FTP browser of your choice.

2. Connect to your hosting and select the file `config.php` for editing (you can also copy the file to your local disk for editing and upload it after the following changes have been made).

3. Search `config.php` for the section "URL Settings" and replace:

    ```
    $config['url_rewriting'] = 'none';
    ```

    with

    ```
    $config['url_rewriting'] = 'mod_rewrite';
    ```

4. Close, save, and upload the file back to your web hosting.

5. Further, using FileZilla or any other FTP browser of your choice, open the `doc` directory.

6. Move the `htaccess.txt` file found in the `doc` directory to the root directory of your website (it is the same directory where the file `config.php` is present).

7. Rename the moved file to `.htaccess` (the period at the beginning belongs to the new filename!).

8. View your website in a browser, click on the top navigation area to see the new addresses for each page.

What just happened?

I am not going to bother you with technical stuff (please read about the `mod_rewrite` module if you would like to know more). You now have some pretty, clean URLs on your website.

If you have received an internal server error, then please consider the following known issues:

◆ Your hosting company does not support `mod_rewrite` (ask your hosting provider if you are not sure).

◆ You have installed CMS Made Simple into a subdirectory; for example, `http://yourdomain.com/mycms`. In this case, you will have to edit the file `.htaccess` and replace the line.

```
RewriteBase /
```

with

```
RewriteBase /mycms
```

Change the name after the slash to your subdirectory's name.

Getting more success from hierarchy

Enabling search engine friendly URLs has another useful effect. The URL of the page now contains the full path to the page including the parent page and not only the page alias.

Let's assume that you have created the page Philips TV (with page alias philips) and selected the page Plasma TV (with page alias plasma-tv) to be the parent page for it. Without rewriting the URL of the page, Philips TV gets the following address:

```
http://yourdomain.com/index.php?page=philips
```

After rewriting the URL of the page, we get:

```
http://yourdomain.com/plasma-tv/philips
```

The second version is cleaner, looks better for visitors, can easily be written down or remembered, and is better for search engines as you also have more keywords in your URL.

However, if you need the same alias twice in the different hierarchy levels, you can use the field Page URL on the tab Options while editing the page.

The alias *products* can be used only once on the entire website.

If your hosting provider does not support `mod_rewrite`, then I recommend leaving them. Seriously, most web hosts have got this feature enabled by default, even free web hosting. There is no reason for not enabling it, unless the provider is not able to install it. Another reason for disabling `mod_rewrite` is that the module is quite processor-intensive, so hosts that put thousands of clients on one server would disable it to gain server performance. These are the reasons why you would not consider such a host and look for another one.

Controlling the navigation of the website

You have seen that the navigation is built automatically from the pages you have created. However, you can interfere in this process and prevent specific pages from displaying the main navigation even if they are on the top level in the page hierarchy.

Time for action – preventing pages from displaying in the navigation

In our company website, we would like to hide the pages **Privacy Policy** and **Sitemap** from the main navigation providing special links to these pages only in the footer navigation later on.

1. In the admin console, click on **Content | Pages**.

2. In the list of pages, click on the page **Privacy Policy** to open it for editing.

3. Switch to the **Options** tab on the top of the editing window and deselect **Show in Menu**, as shown in the following screenshot.

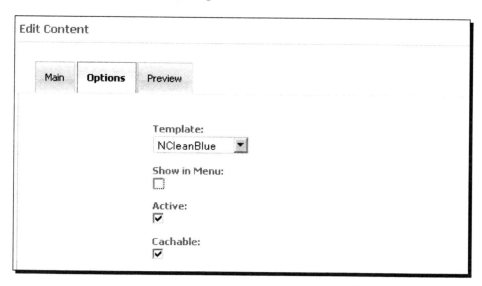

4. Scroll down to the bottom of the page, and click on the **Submit** button.

5. View your website with the magnifier icon on the top right of the admin console.

Do the same for the **Sitemap** page.

What just happened?

You have deselected **Show in Menu** to hide the page from the main navigation of your website. The link to the page disappears from the top menu.

However, the page is not deactivated. You can still view it if you enter the full address of the page in the address bar of your browser or place a direct link to it from other pages of your website. Normally you would use this feature to hide pages that are not important enough to be shown in the main navigation.

Another reason can be that specific pages have to be displayed only under certain circumstances. An example for such a page can be a *Thank you!* page that has to be displayed to the visitor when he sends us a message using the contact form on the website. We speak about service pages in this case.

On the **Options** tab, you may have noticed another field that can be deselected: **Active**. Deactivating a page makes it unavailable to the visitors of the website. Even if a direct link is given to the page, the visitor will see an error message saying that the page could not be found.

 Think of pages that are not active as pages that do not exist as far as visitors are concerned.

You can use this feature to disable a page that you do not need any more. You can delete such pages and lose the contents of them or just deactivate them, while still being able to see their content in the admin console of your website. In this case, you are the only person who can see it. Some webmasters create inactive pages as a placeholder for future content.

What is your start page?

When your website is published online, individual pages can be reached through their links. But what page is displayed to the visitor if only the domain name of your website is given?

In CMS Made Simple, we call this the **default page**. You can define any page to be the default one. In the admin console, open **Content | Pages** and find the column **Default** in the list of current pages. Only one page has a green tick in the column and the page marked in this way is the start page of your website. You can choose another page to be the default page by clicking on the red cross in the column. Before the default page is changed, you have to confirm the question **Are you sure you want to set** (Page name) **as site default page?** See how the green tick is now moved from the previous default page to the new one. The previous page shows a red cross automatically in the column. Logically, you can have only one start page for your website.

More navigation control with content types

More control over your navigation can be achieved with different content types. You have surely noticed the **Content Type** field on the screen where the page is created or edited. The standard choice in this field is **Content** that is used to create an ordinary content page. You use this type in most cases.

With different content types (refer to the following table), you can add links to your navigation and get other behavior than ordinary pages.

Content type	Description
Internal page link	Use this content type to create a link in navigation to a specific page that is actually at another level of hierarchy. This content type generates just a link to the specific page that you select in the field **Destination page**.
Separator	Use this content type to internally separate different navigation sections from each other. This content type is mostly used to create sophisticated navigation structures or complex navigation design.
Redirecting Link	As the name of the content type suggests, add an external link with this content type to your navigation. Enter complete URL starting with http:// in the field **URL** of the content type.
Error page	This content type does not deal with navigation.
Section header	With this content type, you create a header in the navigation. This content type is not a link itself. It just "holds" other pages placed below it in the hierarchy. You use this content type to visibly divide your menu structure into different parts.
Content	This content type is used as standard for normal content pages of your website.

Efficient work with pages

You have noticed that if you create a new page some fields are predefined; for example, the new page is active and shown in the menu. Page-specific metadata is prefilled with a comment:

```
<!-- Add code here that should appear in the metadata section of all
new pages -->
```

You can change the predefined values in the admin console. In the admin console, click on **Site Admin | Page Defaults** and set the fields the way you would like them to be set if a new page is created.

You can predefine meta tags and even the content field of the page. For example, you can create empty meta tags, which are shown as follows:

```
<meta name="keywords" content="" />
<meta name="description" content="" />
```

Now, the editor of the content has to just fill the content attribute of the meta tags (between the quotes) while creating or editing pages.

Creating a new page as a copy of existing one

You can create a new page as a copy of an existing page. In the list of current pages in the admin console (**Content | Pages**), you will find an icon for copy on the left-hand side. Click on the icon to see the next window. It is divided into two sections. The above section called **Copy From** shows the data of the page you are going to copy. You cannot change any data in it. In the section below (**Copy To**), you can enter the page alias, title, and menu text. Select another parent page for the copy if it differs from the original. Click on **Submit** and a new page is created.

New pages created as a copy do not connect to the original page in any way. You can now edit the new page the same way you would do it with other pages. You can also delete it without affecting the original page.

Changing multiple pages at once

If you have a large number of pages and would like to change more than one page at once, then you can use bulk actions in CMS Made Simple.

In the list of the current pages in the admin console (**Content | Pages**), select the checkboxes on the right-hand side of each page that has to be changed, then choose the desired action in the **With selected** field at the bottom of the page. You can activate them, show them in menu, and perform some other actions.

Pop quiz – creating pages and navigation

1. How do you create new pages in CMS Made Simple?

    a. **Site Admin | Page Defaults | Add new page.**

    b. **Layout | Menu Manager | Add new page.**

    c. **Content | Pages | Add New Content.**

2. Where is the title that you fill in when creating a new page shown on the website?

    a. Title bar and menu.

    b. Title bar and heading of the site.

    c. Menu and submenu.

    d. Menu and head of the site.

3. What are the right answers considering the buttons **Apply** and **Submit**?

    a. The **Submit** button saves changes and closes the page in one step.

    b. The **Apply** button saves changes and closes the page in one step.

    c. The **Submit** button does not close the page; but saves the changes you have made.

    d. The **Submit** button does not close the page and previews the changes in the browser.

4. What will be affected if the page alias is changed?

    a. Title

    b. Keywords

    c. Menu

    d. URL

5. Where do you place the meta tags that are valid for all pages in the project?

    a. **Content | Pages | Page Title | Options.**

    b. In the section general meta tags of the stylesheet.

    c. **Site Admin | Global Settings | General Settings | Global Metadata.**

    d. **Extensions | Module Manager | GenMetaMod.**

6. Why should you use search engine friendly addresses?

    a. The RAM memory of your computer gets an overload by opening more than seven pages without search engine friendly URLs (they are too long).

    b. The URL is optimized for search engines.

    c. You should not use them at all, because you have to create a special one for every search engine, and create some duplicate content.

    d. The page is loaded much quicker.

7. If you would like to hide a page from visitors but do want to keep the content on the page for internal needs, you should:

    a. Delete the page.

    b. Deactivate the page.

    c. Assign another parent page.

    d. Copy the page and delete the original.

8. All your pages are written in English. Where would you put the meta tag for the language?

    a. In global settings.

    b. In every single page.

9. One of your pages has been linked to another website. What happens if you change the page alias?

    a. Old link will be redirected to the new page alias automatically.

    b. An error message that the page cannot be found appears after clicking on the link.

Have a go hero – create all pages for company website

Before proceeding create all the pages you need for your website. You do not need to write the entire text for each page of the website.

Use your own website plan or the sample one:

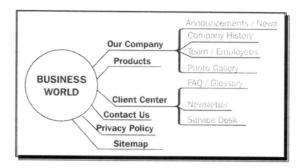

Creating pages and navigation

First add pages that are on the first level in your hierarchy (marked in bold in the preceding diagram). Then add the pages from the second level (marked in grey). You can adjust the page alias and menu text.

Add some sample text to the pages or write down what each single page will contain. If you have some ideas that are nice but should not be available on the website from the very beginning, then create some inactive pages holding these ideas.

Do not create more than two levels at the beginning. Even though it is possible to create a large number of levels, your visitors will find the navigation of the website more user friendly if they do not have to click 5 or 6 times to reach the desired information.

The result of the website structure presented above is as follows:

Please note that the **Start** page has been renamed to **Our Company**.

Summary

In this chapter, you learned how easily pages can be created and managed. You saw that the navigation of your website is built automatically from the existing pages.

Specifically, we covered the following:

- ◆ **Creating pages**: You can create new pages from scratch or as a copy of an existing page.

- ◆ **Editing pages**: You can change everything on the page after it has been created, such as title, content, menu text, or page alias.

- ◆ **Adding meta tags**: Meta tags can be defined globally, if they are the same for each page. For individual meta tags on each specific page, you use the field **Page Specific Metadata** in the **Options** tab.

- ◆ **Page hierarchy**: Pages can be organized in a tree hierarchy. It helps to keep your pages structured and control the top and subnavigation of the website intuitively.

- ◆ **Search engine friendly URLs**: You modified the URLs for your pages. It gives you clean and pretty URLs that are quite noticeable for the visitors too.

- ◆ **Navigation control**: Pages are displayed automatically in the navigation. You can control this behavior by hiding the pages from navigation (they are still accessible by the visitors with direct links). You can also set the page to inactive so that only you, as the website administrator, are able to see the content of the links.

We also discussed how you create or change the start page of your website, gain more control by using different content types, or change multiple pages at once to save time.

Pop Quiz Answers

Chapter 3: Creating Pages and Navigation

1	c
2	b
3	a
4	c
5	c
6	b
7	b
8	a
9	b

Index

Thank you for buying
CMS Made Simple 1.9 Beginner's Guide: LITE

About Packt Publishing

Packt, pronounced 'packed', published its first book "*Mastering phpMyAdmin for Effective MySQL Management*" in April 2004 and subsequently continued to specialize in publishing highly focused books on specific technologies and solutions.

Our books and publications share the experiences of your fellow IT professionals in adapting and customizing today's systems, applications, and frameworks. Our solution based books give you the knowledge and power to customize the software and technologies you're using to get the job done. Packt books are more specific and less general than the IT books you have seen in the past. Our unique business model allows us to bring you more focused information, giving you more of what you need to know, and less of what you don't.

Packt is a modern, yet unique publishing company, which focuses on producing quality, cutting-edge books for communities of developers, administrators, and newbies alike. For more information, please visit our website: www.packtpub.com.

About Packt Open Source

In 2010, Packt launched two new brands, Packt Open Source and Packt Enterprise, in order to continue its focus on specialization. This book is part of the Packt Open Source brand, home to books published on software built around Open Source licences, and offering information to anybody from advanced developers to budding web designers. The Open Source brand also runs Packt's Open Source Royalty Scheme, by which Packt gives a royalty to each Open Source project about whose software a book is sold.

Writing for Packt

We welcome all inquiries from people who are interested in authoring. Book proposals should be sent to author@packtpub.com. If your book idea is still at an early stage and you would like to discuss it first before writing a formal book proposal, contact us; one of our commissioning editors will get in touch with you.

We're not just looking for published authors; if you have strong technical skills but no writing experience, our experienced editors can help you develop a writing career, or simply get some additional reward for your expertise.

LITE Code: IUR72760E252

Drupal 7

ISBN: 978-1-849512-86-2   Paperback: 416 pages

Create and operate any type of Drupal 7 website
quickly and efficiently

1. Set up, configure, and deploy a Drupal 7 website

2. Easily add exciting and powerful features

3. Design and implement your website's look and feel

4. Promote, manage, and maintain your live website

WordPress 3 Complete

ISBN: 978-1-84951-410-1   Paperback: 344 pages

Create your own complete website or blog from
scratch with WordPress

1. Learn everything you need for creating your own
   feature-rich website or blog from scratch

2. Clear and practical explanations of all aspects of
   WordPress

3. In-depth coverage of installation, themes, plugins,
   and syndication

Please check **www.PacktPub.com** for information on our titles

CPSIA information can be obtained at www.ICGtesting.com
Printed in the USA
BVOW061506250911

272035BV00003B/176/P